THE LITTLE BOOK OF

LIVING FRUGAL

Written by Dr. Charlotte Gorman

Illustrated by Peter Standley

**Andrews McMeel
Publishing, LLC**

Kansas City · Sydney · London

10 11 12 13 14 WKT 10 9 8 7 6 5 4 3 2 1

ISBN-13: 978-0-7407-9136-9
ISBN-10: 0-7407-9136-2

Library of Congress Control Number: 2009939464

First published in the United Kingdom by Nightingale Press, BATH, BA2 3LR

www.andrewsmcmeel.com

ATTENTION: SCHOOLS AND BUSINESSES
Andrews McMeel books are available at quantity discounts with bulk purchase for educational, business, or sales promotional use. For information, please write to: Special Sales Department, Andrews McMeel Publishing, LLC, 1130 Walnut Street, Kansas City, Missouri 64106.

Frugality is defined as "wise economy in the management of money and other resources." Being frugal is not being cheap, miserly, or stingy. It is simply avoiding the unnecessary expenditure of money, that is, being "thrifty." Every penny saved is income multiplied. The more you save, the more you will want to save—until frugality becomes a happy and rewarding way of life.

—Dr. Charlotte Gorman

SAVING ON
AUTOMOBILE EXPENSES

So you want a new car? Have you thought about checking out this year's model "demonstrator" automobile or program car with a very low mileage? You should be able to buy it much cheaper than a comparable "new" model. In addition to initial savings on the purchase price, the "demonstrator" should require fewer trips to the dealership for minor repairs and adjustments, since, hopefully, it has received regular professional care and maintenance. Generally you can expect that the "demonstrator" will carry the full "new" automobile warranty—insist on it.

When you are shopping for a car, truck, or van, think about buying one with only the features, optional equipment, and accessories you really need and want. For example, if you rarely drive outside the city, you shouldn't pay the added cost for cruise control. If you don't really need an air conditioner, why pay for it? Not only does an air conditioner cost hundreds of dollars, it also adds to the weight of the vehicle, and reduces fuel economy, thus using up valuable natural resources.

If you are looking for a used vehicle to buy, why not visit car rental agencies? Normally, their automobiles have been regularly serviced and properly maintained for customer use, which could save you money on repairs and time at the repair shop.

Before you purchase a used automobile, remember to have a reputable mechanic whom you know and trust (one not connected with the dealer, other agency, or individual who has the automobile for sale) evaluate the vehicle for you. The charge for this service is usually low. The examination could save you from buying an automobile with serious problems or potential problems. It may also point out several minor problems that can be corrected easily and could be used to reduce the asking price.

When you are thinking about buying an automobile, consider how much your insurance on it will cost. Some vehicles, especially luxury cars, are very expensive to insure. Also, because of such factors as age and/or driving record of the operator, insurance rates could be extremely high for some people. You will want to make sure you will be able to afford the insurance before you purchase the vehicle. If you purchase the vehicle and later realize that you can't keep up the insurance payments, ownership can become a serious problem.

Have you ever thought about installing your own automobile air filters? They are simple to install. You could save up to 50 percent on the "service station" charge. When you find filters on sale at a very good price, you will probably want to buy several at one time and reap the savings.

Frugality is a handsome income.

—Erasmus

You don't have to be a trained mechanic to do simple automobile repairs yourself. A large part of the cost of automobile repairs is for labor—often as much as 90 percent of the final bill. A small investment in a short course on automobile maintenance and repair could pay for itself many times over, in a short period of time.

When you use self-service gas pumps, don't forget to check such things as your automobile's oil level, brake fluid level, transmission fluid level, radiator water level, windshield washer reservoir level, and tire pressure. Neglecting these things could result in expensive problems for you and your vehicle, and possibly leave you stranded out on the road.

It's better to be safe than sorry. Before freezing weather, remind yourself to fill your automobile's windshield washer reservoir with a non-freezing cleaner solution. Otherwise, your ordinary solution will freeze and will not be usable when needed. In this case, mud or slush splashed onto your windshield could cause a serious accident. Accidents are bad for your health and your finances!

If and when you take your automobile to a shop, make sure you ask that any guarantees related to repairs or services be put in writing. If you have repairs or services done at national chain stores or shops, remember to keep copies of all bills and guarantees in your vehicle, should you have trouble with these same problems while you are away from home. Verbal guarantees are risky and could leave you out of pocket when trouble arises with the same problem.

Before you take your automobile to a shop for service or repair, do you prepare a written, dated, and signed list (keep a copy for yourself) of repairs or services you want done on your automobile to leave with the mechanic? If you don't leave such a list, you could return and find some of the things you wanted done left undone; or you might find charges on your bill for things you did not authorize. Also, ask for a written estimate of the costs. Otherwise, you might receive a bill for twice the amount you expected to pay.

Sunshine is free, but it can be expensive. If you don't have a carport or garage, explore the possibility of purchasing a flexible covering to protect your vehicle from the sun. The sun can fade the outside paint and the inside upholstery. It can, also, over an extended period of time, weaken the upholstery and cause it to deteriorate. Lack of protection from the sun could create a need for a premature paint job or replacement of upholstery—each of which represents money out of your pocket.

Washing your car regularly does more than create a cosmetic effect. It helps to preserve the finish. Follow the automobile manufacturer's instructions on washing and waxing. A vehicle whose finish has been well preserved should bring more money when it is traded or sold, and it will look better while you are driving it, too.

Think about where you park your car. Be careful about parking it under trees that drip sap or in which birds roost. The paint on your car could be ruined, and a new paint job is costly.

Accidents cost money and often cause serious injuries. Try to drive defensively to reduce the possibility of having an accident. Be on the alert and pay attention to your driving at all times when you are behind the wheel. An accident may cost you some money even if you have automobile insurance and health insurance and even if it isn't your fault. Also, many people are reluctant to buy a vehicle that has been in an accident.

Can you find a way to cut down on the number of shopping trips you make? Can you plan your shopping so that you can run all of your errands in fewer trips? Can you combine trips? Driving to run errands many times a week can become very expensive in terms of gas use and wear and tear on your automobile, not to mention polluting the environment.

How long does it take to warm up your automobile before you take it onto the road or street? Research tells us that automobile warm-ups should not exceed one minute. The gas consumed in long warm-ups is not offset by any great improvement in engine performance.

Mend your clothes and you may hold
out this year.

—George Herbert

Ah, make the most of what we yet
may spend.

—Edward Fitzgerald

Many people don't realize that they should turn off the ignition if they stop for more than one minute. (This does not apply when you are "in traffic.") Restarting the automobile will use less gas than idling for more than one minute. Drivers shouldn't wait until they unbuckle their seat belt, turn off their lights, turn off their air conditioner, gather items from the seat to take with them, etc., before they turn off the engine. When the engine stops, gas costs stop; and an important natural resource is saved.

Think about taking your vacation near home this year. Most of us fail to see and enjoy the attractions in our own area. Instead, we tend to drive long distances for a vacation. People hundreds of miles away drive to see our attractions, and we drive to their attractions even though we haven't seen our own nor have they seen their own. Discover some exciting things close to home this year and save hundreds of dollars in transportation costs.

Have you removed unnecessary weight from the trunk of your automobile? Generally, the lighter the vehicle, the less gas it will use. An extra 100 pounds decreases fuel economy by about 1 percent for the average car, and 1.25 percent for a small car.

Why don't you give this a try?
Order needed items over the telephone
or Internet and have the items delivered. The overall delivered cost of the
items is usually less than the price of
the items on the shelf plus the cost of
the drive combined.

If you have never carpooled, you might be surprised at the amount of money you can save. Drive your automobile only part of the time to and from work and to various other activities. For example, if you could carpool with just one other person, you could save 50 percent on the cost of gas for getting to and from work. Carpool with three others and save 75 percent. And perhaps more importantly, you will reduce your contribution to air pollution and the unnecessary waste of gas.

SAVING ON CLOTHING EXPENSES

When you are considering the purchase of some item of clothing, have you thought of asking yourself, "Do I really need that garment?" "Do I really need a new white shirt, or will the ten white ones I already own be sufficient?" "Should I buy another business suit with ten good business suits hanging in my closet?" An answer of "no" to these and similar questions can save you money—money you can put into your savings account or use for other purposes.

Do you always make a list of the clothes you need to buy? It's easy to buy on impulse. Even if certain items are on sale, do you resist the temptation to purchase them if they are not on your "needs" list? For example, as a business executive, you have on your list the following items: a solid navy suit and a solid medium gray suit. Don't buy a white suit and a red jacket, instead, just because they are on sale and you think they look good on you.

If you have never shopped garage/yard sales, you are missing out on one of the greatest money-saving activities. Before I purchase any item of clothing, I shop the garage/yard sales first. Clothes will almost always be much cheaper there than anywhere else. By shopping garage/yard sales, I have reduced my clothing expenditures by 98 percent. Garage/yard sales usually are excellent places to find baby and children's clothes that often show very little wear and cost only a fraction of the price charged in stores for comparable new clothes.

Buying previously worn clothing is rapidly becoming an accepted practice in all segments of society. The stigma once attached to wearing secondhand clothing has all but disappeared. Today, people are admired for finding a used bargain. A number of prominent people I know purchase many of their clothes secondhand from thrift shops.

If you can't bring yourself to buy clothes at garage/yard sales, you might want to check stores that sell previously worn clothing. Clothes are almost always much cheaper at these stores than they can be purchased new at "new" stores. Such clothing stores might be called thrift shops, second-hand shops, used clothing stores, resale shops, clothing exchanges, or second-time-around shops. Try these stores for men's, women's, children's, and baby clothes. Some shops even specialize in designer clothes.

Are you open to the purchasing of "seconds" or "irregulars" with very minor flaws? If the flaws are not noticeable to others and do not decrease the comfort or durability of the garments, you can save a great deal of money and no one will ever know the difference. Start with purchasing one or two items. "Seconds" and "irregulars" are normally much cheaper than comparable "first-quality" garments.

If you buy most of your clothes new, try buying them only when they are on sale, preferably 50 percent or more off. It usually is only a matter of time until most clothes go on sale. It should be a very rare occasion when you will need to pay the full price for a garment. End-of-the-season sales are ideal for stocking up your wardrobe. Once you see how much money you save, you will never want to pay full price again.

Try to limit your purchases of clothing decorated with frilly lace or other trimmings that may wear out before the rest of the garment. Especially limit such ornamentation on children's clothes, since children are "rough" on clothes and the trimmings will be even more susceptible to wear and tear. If you do buy clothes with ornamentation, make sure it is sturdy enough to last as long as the garment itself. Otherwise, you could find yourself having to replace the clothing prematurely.

Is your clothes closet bulging with "fad" clothing that you will never wear again? If so, consider cutting back on your purchases of these types of garments. "Fads" usually go out of style in a year or less. Having to buy a new wardrobe each year could get relatively expensive. If you do purchase a "fad" garment, spend as little as possible on it.

If you buy most of your clothes in simple, classic, basic, traditional, and conservative styles that will stay in style for many years, your overall clothing expenses through the years should be much less. Why buy clothes that don't feel good on you? If you have doubts about a garment, don't buy it. If it doesn't feel good on you, you will never be completely happy with it; and you probably will wear it very rarely. You will have wasted your money, and the garment will only be taking up space in your closet.

Industry, perseverance, and frugality
make fortune yield.

—Benjamin Franklin

Who likes to iron clothes? A wise shopper looks for wash-and-wear, permanent press, and wrinkle-resistant clothing whenever possible. Washing is cheaper than dry cleaning. Permanent press clothing will require little or no ironing. Wrinkle-resistant clothing will need little or no pressing between wearings. Save your money and your valuable time for other pursuits.

If you discover mildew on clothes or shoes in your closet, remove the mildew as soon as possible. Try one or more of the following to prevent any further mildew: Leave the closet doors open to allow air to circulate and to admit light. Leave an electric light burning in the closet to provide light: It might also provide enough heat to keep moisture down. Place a chemical moisture absorber in the closet. If neglected, mildew can ruin your clothes or shoes; and replacements cost money.

Be careful where you sit. Check to make sure that where you are going to sit is not dirty or greasy. You might want to keep a couple of paper towels in your briefcase or purse to wipe off a seat when there is a need. Sitting in a soiled seat may cost you a dry-cleaning bill or ruin your garment.

Discarded garments can be cut up and used as cleaning and dusting rags. For example, a 100 percent cotton man's vest makes an excellent dusting rag. Utilizing discarded garments saves you the cost of buying cleaning and dusting cloths and contributes to your recycling efforts.

Have you thought about having your own garage/yard sale to sell clothes you no longer wish to wear? Garage/yard sales are growing in popularity and have become regular weekend outings and forms of recreation for many people. You could make extra money from the sale and clean out your closet, too.

Economy is the science of avoiding
unnecessary expenditure, or the art
of using one's income with moderation.
                                    —Seneca

He will always be a slave who does
not know how to live upon a little.

—Horace

If you have nice, stylish clothes in your closet that you do not plan to wear again, consider placing them in a consignment shop. The clothes should be clean and in good shape. (You get a percentage of the money from the sales, if and when the clothes sell. Items unsold after a specified length of time are returned to the owner.)

Have you ever done an inventory of the clothes hanging in your closet to determine whether some of them might qualify for sale as "vintage" clothing? If you find some that qualify, why not sell them to a "vintage" clothing store? These stores sell "antique" clothes that are 20, 30, and 40 years old. (These clothes usually command a higher price than newer, used clothes.)

Need a new pair of shoes? Think about buying a pair of shoes in a color and style that can be worn with many of your clothes, not just one particular garment. The more clothes with which you can wear a pair of shoes, the fewer pairs of shoes you should need. And think of the money and closet space you will save.

For age and want save while you may;
no morning sun lasts a whole day.

—Benjamin Franklin

SAVING ON ENERGY EXPENSES

Try setting your home temperature thermostat between 64 and 70 degrees F in the winter during the day and between 78 and 80 degrees F in the summer during the day. Experiment—you may be able to adjust the setting down or up even a few more degrees and still be comfortable. Each degree makes a difference in the utility bill, in addition to conserving energy.

If you plan to buy a new electric heating/cooling system, consider installing a heat pump for heating and cooling your house. Research shows that a heat pump can cut your use of electricity for heating by 30 to 40 percent and also might provide some savings in cooling costs. Ask experts about the possible benefits of using a heat pump in your geographical area.

Be sure to remember to turn off the gas furnace pilot light during the summer. The pilot light uses gas; thus, it increases your gas bill and wastes energy needlessly.

He that buys by the penny,
maintains not only himself, but
other people.

—Benjamin Franklin

He who spends all he gets is on the way to beggary.

—Samuel Smiles

Use kitchen and bathroom ventilating fans sparingly during cold weather (also in hot weather if the air conditioner is running). In just one hour, these fans can blow away a houseful of heated or cooled air. Turn them off just as soon as they have done their jobs and save money on recooling and reheating.

If you are using a window air conditioner to cool a room, don't forget to turn it off if you are going to leave the room for several hours. Research has shown that less energy will be required to recool the room than the unit will use if you leave it running. You will conserve energy and save on your electric bill.

Ceiling or portable fans can be used to enhance your air-conditioning unit. The fans help circulate the air and make the higher temperatures feel cooler. As a result, you should be able to raise your thermostat setting a bit and still feel as comfortable as you would at a lower setting without using fans. Each degree you raise the thermostat setting makes a difference in your cooling expenses.

This may be difficult for you, but try sleeping without covering at night in warm or hot weather. It is a waste of energy and money to cover up with a sheet, a blanket, and maybe even a bedspread, and then lower the thermostat setting so you won't be too warm under all of that covering. The less covering you use, the less cooling you will need, thus, the less energy you will use.

In warm and hot weather, you can keep the heat of the sun out of your home by using awnings on the outside of windows or placing reflective film on the inside and/or by closing draperies, blinds, shades, or other inside window coverings in sunny windows. Keeping the sunshine out will decrease the need for mechanical cooling and reduce your electric bill.

You can save money on water heating by reducing the temperature setting on your water heater to the lowest effective and acceptable temperature. Most owners' manuals recommend a setting no higher than 120 degrees F for most household uses. Research has shown that keeping the water heater setting at 120 degrees F can save 18 percent of the energy used compared to a setting of 140 degrees F. Each degree rise in temperature setting increases your energy bill.

Cold water is usually cheaper than hot water. Make an effort to use water from the cold water tap for doing as many of your household tasks as possible. Heating water costs money.

Sediment in your water heater reduces its efficiency and increases your energy bill. Drain the sediment (about four quarts of water) from the bottom of your water heater at least twice a year. Attach a garden hose to the water heater tap, which is near the bottom of the tank, and run the hose to the outside of the house. Then, open the tap to run off the water.

You'll save money if you keep the coils on the backs of your refrigerator and freezer clean. Dusty coils require the appliances to work harder and, thus, use more energy, which costs money.

Do you attempt to keep your refrigerator no colder than recommended (38 to 40 degrees F for the fresh food compartment and 5 degrees F for the freezer compartment)? If you have a separate freezer for long-term storage, it should be kept at 0 degrees F. You can use an ordinary thermometer (not a medical one) for checking the temperatures. It is a waste of money and energy to keep these appliances colder than necessary.

Have you ever tried opening your dish-washer door after the final rinse cycle and letting dishes air dry naturally? You could save the cost of the electric-ity required to operate the drying cycle.

Consider using water from the cold water tap rather than from the hot water tap when operating the garbage disposer. Not only does the cold water save the money and the energy needed to heat the water, but the cold water aids in getting rid of grease. The grease solidifies in cold water and can be ground up and washed away.

Think about installing dimmer switches. If you already have them, remember to use them. Dimmers make it easy to reduce the lighting intensity in a room and, therefore, save energy and money.

You can save water by installing a showerhead flow restrictor or a low-flow showerhead in your shower outlet. Either of these can reduce the flow of water from 6 to 8 gallons per minute for a conventional showerhead down to 2 to 3 gallons per minute. The less hot water used, the less energy used.

Resolve not to be poor; whatever you have, spend less.

—Samuel Johnson

He who will not lay up a penny shall never have many.

—Thomas Fuller

Sometimes it is hard to remember,
but if you turn off televisions, radios,
stereos, etc., when no one is watching
or listening to them, you will save
considerable energy and money.

Keeping the cutting edges sharp on gas and electric-powered yard equipment will not only save you valuable time, but the equipment will cut more efficiently and, therefore, use less energy. Energy costs money.

If you are in the market for a major appliance, you will find it to your advantage to compare the energy consumption of similar models to determine which model is the most energy efficient. The information should be listed on a label attached to each model. The most energy-efficient model will be cheaper to operate and, even if it costs more to purchase it, it will save you money in the long run.

Frugality enhances all other virtues.
                              —Cicero

You don't have to "hang it out to dry," but have you thought about letting your hair dry naturally lately? You could save the cost of electricity needed to run the hair dryer.

SAVING ON
FOOD EXPENSES

Have you tried planning your weekly menus around the grocery store "specials"? It is possible to limit most of your food purchases to only the "specials." Check out the "specials" list in circulars and in the food section of your newspaper. You should not have to pay full price for very many food items if you plan well. Most food items normally will be on sale sometime during a period of several months. By concentrating on the "specials," you should be able to save a sizable amount on your weekly grocery bill.

There is something good to be said about preparing a written shopping list before you go grocery shopping. A shopping list will help you to avoid unwise impulse buying. It will help you buy only what is on your grocery list unless you find outstanding, unadvertised "specials" on items that you can use (this is wise impulse buying) and cheaper substitutions for items on your list.

Try hard to restrict your food purchases at convenience stores. There is usually a wide gap between the prices on most food items here as compared to the prices at traditional grocery stores.

"What's in a name?" When grocery shopping, you will want to compare the prices of national brands, store brands, "off" brands, and generic (no-name) labels of a particular food. Buy the cheapest one (which is usually the generic label). We shouldn't just assume that the most expensive brand is necessarily the best.

If your grocery store has sold out of the "advertised special" that enticed you to the store in the first place, don't forget to ask the manager if a comparable item can be substituted, and, if not, don't hesitate to ask for a rain check. Most stores will either substitute or give a rain check.

Unless you have a medical problem that requires you to buy certain, special "diet" offers, try to limit your purchases of these foods. They are almost always more expensive than "ordinary" foods.

Try purchasing meats, poultry, and fish by "cost per serving." Consider how much wastage (bone, fat, gristle) there will be. In other words, how many edible servings can you get from one pound of the particular meat, poultry, or fish you are considering? Figuring the "cost per serving" will help you to get the most edible food at the lowest price.

Have you used alternatives (substitutes) for meat, poultry or fish, such as dry beans and peas, cheese, peanut butter, nuts, and eggs, at some meals? These protein alternates are usually less expensive per serving. Do we really need all that meat anyway?

If you want to save money on cereals, choose the large boxes or bags of ready-to-eat cereals rather than packages of assorted single-serving boxes, which are usually much more expensive per serving.

You can reduce your grocery bill if you make it a point to shop alone. Spouses, roommates, and especially children may influence you to buy one or more additional items. Or, you may be distracted by the person or persons with you and not concentrate as much on saving on the grocery bill. Therefore, you may spend more money than you might have if you had shopped alone.

Do you ever shop for groceries when you are hungry? People usually will buy more food items, including snack items, when they are hungry. This can wreak havoc with your grocery budget.

All of us are sometimes guilty of wasting food. Instead of throwing it away, we can, for example, use overripe (not spoiled) fruit in cobblers, puddings, congealed desserts, cakes, and pies. We should not allow any of our food to reach the point that it has to be thrown away. Throwing away food is just like throwing money out the window. And it doesn't seem right to throw away food when there are so many hungry people in the world.

Are some of us guilty of leaving left-over foods sitting on the dining table while we clear away and wash the dishes? Foods that need to be refrigerated should be returned to the refrigerator as quickly as possible. Foods left out of the refrigerator too long could spoil and would have to be thrown away.

Think about going to restaurants where you can order half-orders or individual items if you are a light eater. If children are with you when you eat out, ask if a children's menu is available—the prices are usually cheaper. If you have sufficient food left on your plate and if it seems appropriate to do so, ask the waiter or waitress to put it in a doggie bag for you. You are wasting your money if the leftovers are thrown away.

Eating out is often pleasurable, but it can also be expensive. If you plan to eat out, consider lunch rather than dinner, since an identical dish can cost several dollars less during lunchtime. In addition, some restaurants even add a salad, dip, or other item to lunch entrées at no extra cost; the added item would cost extra at dinnertime.

How about going to "happy hours" where free snacks are served? You buy one drink (alcoholic or nonalcoholic) and make your meal on snacks. It is almost unbelievable the array of snacks some places offer. A meal for the price of one drink would be a fairly inexpensive way of eating out. (Don't drive if you have had alcoholic beverages!)

Could your children take their lunches to school if this seems appropriate at your children's school and is less expensive than eating in the school cafeteria or eating out?

SAVING ON WATER EXPENSES

Using less water means saving money, whether you are on a city water line or own your own well. If you are on the city water line, your bills come regularly. If you own your own well, you must take into account the investment you have in your water system, repair and maintenance costs, and the cost of electricity used in operating the pump.

For the average family of four, bathing accounts for 30 percent of the total water used in the home. Consider cutting back on the number of showers and tub baths you take. The ordinary shower, equipped with a conventional showerhead, uses from 5 to 10 gallons of water per minute. Saving water is saving money.

When you buy clothing and household items, try to seek out those that don't have to be washed separately. Washing them separately will require additional use of the clothes washer (unless you wash them by hand), which means additional money for water.

When purchasing a clothes washer, shop around for a model with choices of water levels (small, medium, and large load settings). By merely pressing a button, you can save many quarts of water per load and enjoy a lower water bill.

It may go against your tradition, but you don't have to rinse dishes that go directly from the table into the automatic dishwasher for immediate washing. Scrape off leftover food, place them in your dishwasher, and let it do the rinsing for you. You will not only save time and water, but you will save money.

Do you really have to use running water from the tap to wash vegetables and fruits? Try using a pan of water for these tasks. When you have finished, you can use the water to water plants. Reusing water is like getting double value for your investment.

If you want to save money on your water bill, refrain from using running water to thaw frozen foods. Thaw them in the refrigerator rather than on the kitchen counter to avoid possible spoilage. You will stay healthier and have a lower water bill.

By saving up routine household cleaning jobs, you can do them all at one time and conserve water. Using the same water, start with the lightest soiled surface and end with the heaviest soiled surface. For example, start with the mirrors and end, eventually, with the floors. A few quarts of water saved each time you clean can add up to noticeable savings, money-wise, over time.

Mulching plants in your yard and vegetable garden will help hold moisture in the soil. Try spreading leaves, cut grass, pieces of bark, plastic, or other appropriate materials around the plants. (Make sure that the mulch does not prevent water from soaking into the soil when you do water or when it rains.) The longer you can keep the soil moist through mulching, the less water you will have to use.

Whenever possible, plan to water your lawn, yard plants, and vegetable garden only in the early morning. It is best not to water in the heat of the day, when it is windy, or when the sun is shining brightly. Under these conditions, you waste a large amount of water through evaporation.

Have you tried using a "soaker" hose rather than a sprinkler for watering plants? Less water is required when a "soaker" hose is used because the water is concentrated on the soil nearer the roots; and there is, also, less evaporation. Save water, save money.

Dripping taps waste more water than one can imagine. It costs very little to repair them. Believe it or not, a slow, steady drip (100 drops per minute) wastes 330 gallons of water in a month. That's 3,960 gallons per year. What a waste of money and water!

Leaking water pipes can boost your water bill tremendously. You normally can suspect a leak if you find unexplained dark green patches of grass or a permanently damp area of ground on your property. An unexplained jump in your water bill may also indicate a leak in your water mains. Try to locate leaks and have them repaired as soon as possible.

It may be difficult for you, but try not to let children play with the water hose. Thirty minutes of fun could use up to 185 gallons of water. Even water used for play costs money.

Use a broom to sweep the garage, sidewalks, and driveway. Don't remove debris by hosing it off with water. You could use over 100 gallons of water (a lot of money) in hosing off the driveway.

When you are away from home for more than a day, you might want to turn off the water supply to your outside taps. This will prevent loss of water should someone turn on the outside taps while you are away. Or, you might place locks on the outside taps to prevent someone from turning them on. These precautions could save you from an unexpected rise in your water bill.

All things are cheap to the saving, dear to the wasteful.

—Benjamin Franklin

Beware of little expenses; a small leak
will sink a great ship.

—Benjamin Franklin